THE GREAT
PREHISTORIC
SEARCH

Jane Bingham

Illustrated by Ian Jackson

Designed by Susie McCaffrey

Edited by Felicity Brooks
Scientific consultant: Professor Michael Benton

Contents

Hylonomus was the first known reptile to live on Earth. You can search for five of these early reptiles on pages 10 and 11.

About this book

This book is filled with exciting scenes from prehistoric times. You can use it to learn about dinosaurs and other creatures, but it's also a puzzle book. If you look carefully at the pictures, you'll be able to spot hundreds of prehistoric plants and animals. You can see below how the puzzles work.

This strip tells you when the animals in the picture lived.

Around the edge of the big picture are lots of little pictures.

The writing next to each little picture tells you the name of a creature. It also tells you how many creatures you can find in the big picture.

Although part of this dinosaur is outside the big picture, you should still count it.

You will have to look hard to spot these stegosaurs in the distance.

Sometimes, there are plants and trees to find.

This Ceratosaurus is shown from a different angle than the one in the little picture, but it still counts.

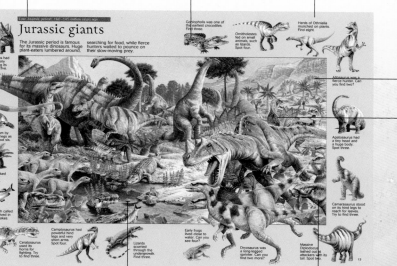
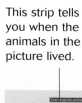

Don't miss this frog, even though it's mainly underwater.

Although you can only see part of this dinosaur, it needs to be counted.

The challenge of these puzzles is to find all the animals and plants in the big picture. Some creatures look very similar so you will need to look carefully to spot the difference. If you get stuck, you can find the answers on pages 28 to 31.

To make the puzzles harder, each big picture shows lots of animals and plants very close together. But the prehistoric world wasn't really as crowded as this.

The prehistoric world

This book covers many millions of years. Its opening scene is set 545 million years ago, when life was just beginning in the oceans. Later came giant insects, fish and amphibians (creatures that could live on land and in water).

Trilobites were some of the first creatures to live in the oceans.

The first dragonflies were as large as seagulls are today.

This early fish swam in prehistoric swamps.

Frog-like amphibians existed 150 million years ago.

The first creatures to spend all their lives on land were reptiles. They had dry, scaly skin and laid eggs. The largest of all the reptiles were the dinosaurs.

Most dinosaurs were enormous. This foot belongs to a dinosaur that was twice the size of elephants today.

Rhamphorhynchus was a flying reptile that scooped up fish in its beak.

About 65 million years ago, all the dinosaurs died out and a new group of animals spread out across the Earth. These were mammals – animals with fur that fed their babies with milk. Gradually, different types of mammals developed around the world.

The first mammals scampered around under the feet of the dinosaurs. They looked like present-day shrews.

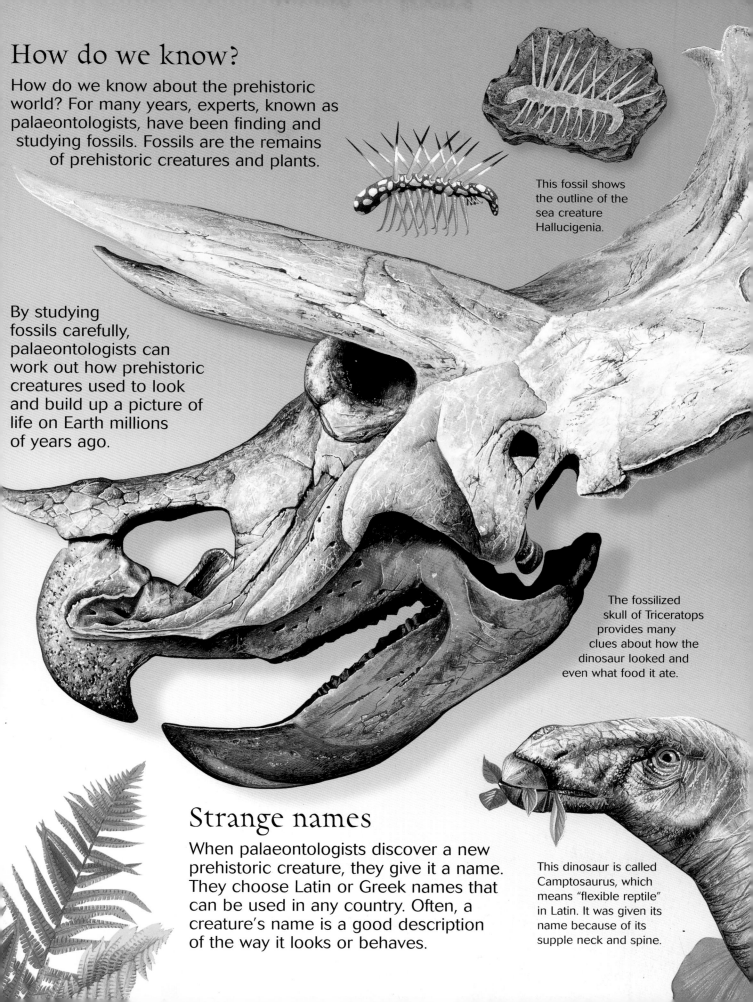

How do we know?

How do we know about the prehistoric world? For many years, experts, known as palaeontologists, have been finding and studying fossils. Fossils are the remains of prehistoric creatures and plants.

This fossil shows the outline of the sea creature Hallucigenia.

By studying fossils carefully, palaeontologists can work out how prehistoric creatures used to look and build up a picture of life on Earth millions of years ago.

The fossilized skull of Triceratops provides many clues about how the dinosaur looked and even what food it ate.

Strange names

When palaeontologists discover a new prehistoric creature, they give it a name. They choose Latin or Greek names that can be used in any country. Often, a creature's name is a good description of the way it looks or behaves.

This dinosaur is called Camptosaurus, which means "flexible reptile" in Latin. It was given its name because of its supple neck and spine.

Prehistoric time

The Earth has existed for billions of years – a length of time so vast it's impossible to imagine. To make it easier to study the Earth's history, experts have divided prehistoric time into different periods. Each period lasted for many millions of years.

This diagram shows the main periods of prehistoric time. You can also see when different animals and plants first appeared on Earth.

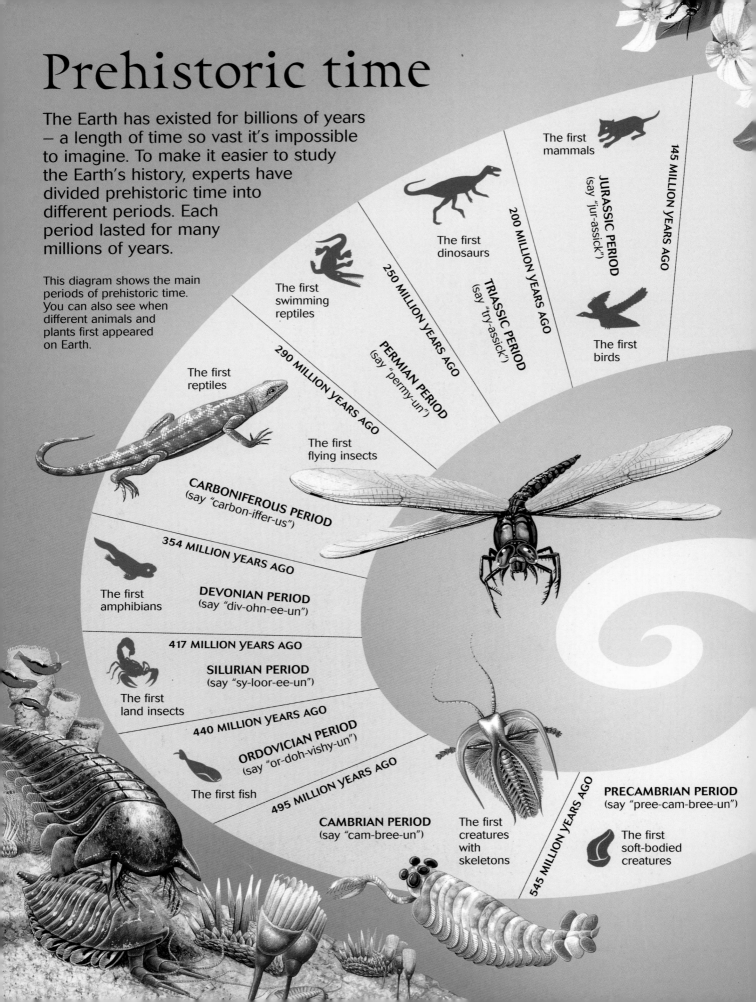

The first mammals

145 MILLION YEARS AGO

JURASSIC PERIOD
(say "jur-assick")

The first birds

The first dinosaurs

200 MILLION YEARS AGO

TRIASSIC PERIOD
(say "try-assick")

The first swimming reptiles

250 MILLION YEARS AGO

PERMIAN PERIOD
(say "perny-un")

The first reptiles

290 MILLION YEARS AGO

The first flying insects

CARBONIFEROUS PERIOD
(say "carbon-iffer-us")

354 MILLION YEARS AGO

The first amphibians

DEVONIAN PERIOD
(say "div-ohn-ee-un")

417 MILLION YEARS AGO

SILURIAN PERIOD
(say "sy-loor-ee-un")

The first land insects

440 MILLION YEARS AGO

ORDOVICIAN PERIOD
(say "or-doh-vishy-un")

The first fish

495 MILLION YEARS AGO

CAMBRIAN PERIOD
(say "cam-bree-un")

The first creatures with skeletons

545 MILLION YEARS AGO

PRECAMBRIAN PERIOD
(say "pree-cam-bree-un")

The first soft-bodied creatures

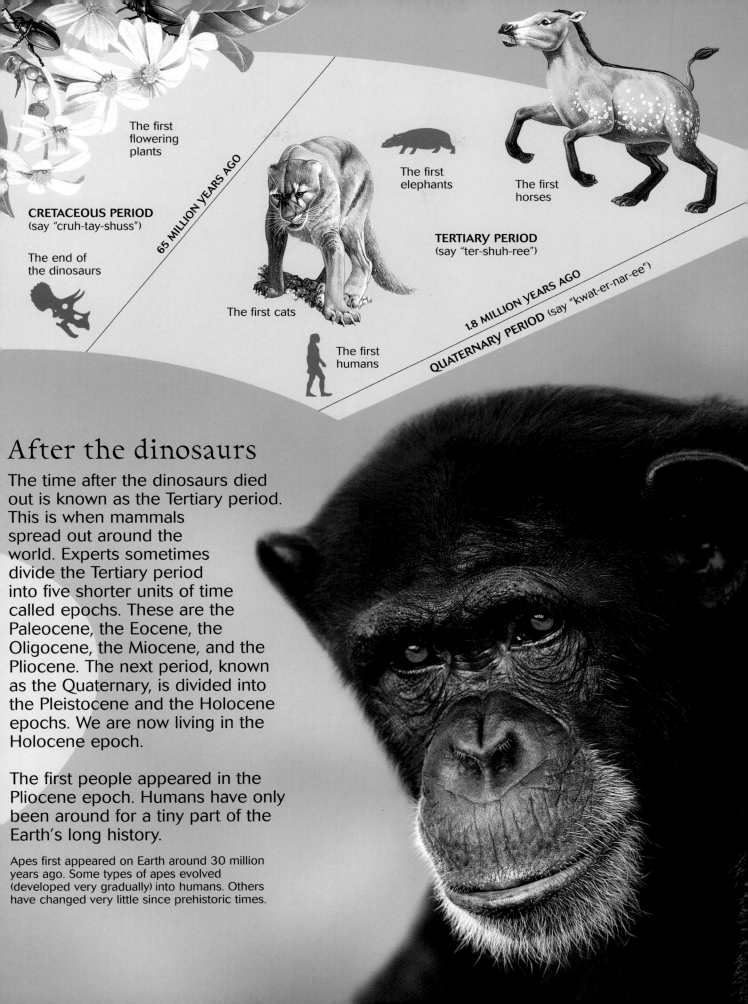

The first
flowering
plants

CRETACEOUS PERIOD
(say "cruh-tay-shuss")

The end of
the dinosaurs

65 MILLION YEARS AGO

The first cats

The first
elephants

The first
horses

TERTIARY PERIOD
(say "ter-shuh-ree")

The first
humans

1.8 MILLION YEARS AGO

QUATERNARY PERIOD (say "kwat-er-nar-ee")

After the dinosaurs

The time after the dinosaurs died
out is known as the Tertiary period.
This is when mammals
spread out around the
world. Experts sometimes
divide the Tertiary period
into five shorter units of time
called epochs. These are the
Paleocene, the Eocene, the
Oligocene, the Miocene, and the
Pliocene. The next period, known
as the Quaternary, is divided into
the Pleistocene and the Holocene
epochs. We are now living in the
Holocene epoch.

The first people appeared in the
Pliocene epoch. Humans have only
been around for a tiny part of the
Earth's long history.

Apes first appeared on Earth around 30 million
years ago. Some types of apes evolved
(developed very gradually) into humans. Others
have changed very little since prehistoric times.

Crowded seas

Around 545 million years ago, an amazing range of creatures began to appear in the oceans. Many of them were protected by shells and spikes. There are 100 creatures for you to find here.

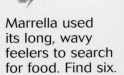

Marrella used its long, wavy feelers to search for food. Find six.

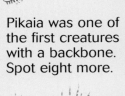

Pikaia was one of the first creatures with a backbone. Spot eight more.

These sponges had long spikes to protect them from hunters. Try finding five.

Transparent jellyfish drifted through the water. Can you spot nine?

Leanchoilia folded its feelers under its body when it swam. Try to find six.

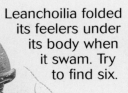

Odontogriphus swam by arching its body up and down. Spot five.

Sanctacaris had 10 claws for crushing its prey. Find four.

8

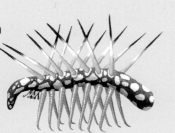

Hallucigenia had two rows of spines on its back. Spot four.

Dinomischus looked like a plant, but it was really an animal. Find 14.

Opabinia had five eyes on stalks and a long nozzle with claws at its tip. Spot three.

Anomalocaris grabbed small creatures in its claws. Can you see one more?

Amiskwia had a flattened body and two small feelers. Spot 10.

Aysheaia had spiky feet for clambering over sponges. Find nine.

Ottoia was a large worm that burrowed into the sea bed. Try to spot four.

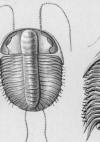

Trilobites scuttled around, searching for food. Find three of each kind.

The shimmering scales of Wiwaxia warned off hunters. Spot six.

9

Forests and swamps

During the Carboniferous period, most of the Earth was covered in steamy forests. Giant insects crawled or flew through the forests, and strange water creatures lurked in swamps.

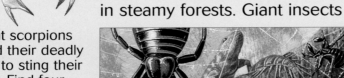

Giant scorpions used their deadly tails to sting their prey. Find four.

Platysomus swam by flicking its body from side to side. Spot 10.

Meganeura was as big as a seagull. Try to find three.

Snake-like Ophiderpeton spent most of its time swimming. Find three.

Arthropleura was a giant millipede that feasted on rotting plants. Spot three.

Cockroaches flew through the air or scuttled over the ground. Find 11.

Eryops looked like a small crocodile. Can you see five?

Early spiders wove simple webs to trap insects. Find four spiders.

Centipedes grasped their prey in their fangs. Spot five.

Keraterpeton used its long tail for swimming. Find six.

Tiny leaves sprouted from the stems of giant horsetails. Spot five.

Sigillaria had no branches, just a clump of leaves. Try to find six.

Towering Lepidodendron had a scaly trunks. Spot six.

Hylonomus is the earliest known reptile. It spent its life on land. Spot five.

Diploceraspis had a head shaped like a boomerang. Try to find four.

Tree ferns were plants that looked like palm trees. Spot three.

11

Jurassic giants

The Jurassic period is famous for its massive dinosaurs. Huge plant-eaters lumbered around, searching for food, while fierce hunters waited to pounce on their slow-moving prey.

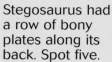

Stegosaurus had a row of bony plates along its back. Spot five.

Turtles swam by using their legs as paddles. Spot six.

Cycads looked a little like pineapples. Find six.

An early fish called Lepidotes lived in rivers and lakes. Spot three.

Ceratosaurus used its horns for fighting. Try to find three.

Camptosaurus had powerful hind legs and very short arms. Spot four.

Lizards scurried through the undergrowth. Find three.

Goniopholis was one of the earliest crocodiles. Find three.

Ornitholestes fed on small animals, such as lizards. Spot four.

Herds of Othnielia munched on plants. Find eight.

Allosaurus was a fierce hunter. Can you find two?

Apatosaurus had a tiny head and a huge body. Spot three.

Camarasaurus stood on its hind legs to reach for leaves. Try to find three.

Early frogs lived close to water. Can you see four?

Dryosaurus was a long-legged sprinter. Can you find two more?

Massive Diplodocus lashed out at attackers with its tail. Spot two.

13

Oceans and skies

At the same time as dinosaurs were living on land, enormous reptiles were swimming through the oceans and swooping through the skies. How many flying and swimming reptiles can you find?

Ichthyosaurus looked like a small dolphin. Try to spot five.

Early shrimps drifted through the water. Find six.

Peloneustes snapped up food in its huge jaws. Spot two.

Fast-flying Anurognathus chased after insects. Find six.

Ammonites were protected by a spiral shell. Spot eight more.

Cryptoclidus had long, flexible flippers. Can you see two?

Aspidorhynchus was an early hunting fish. Spot three.

Pterodactylus had wings like a bat. Spot three more.

Metriorhynchus was an early crocodile with a tail and flippers. Find three.

Belemnites had long, wavy suckers. Can you see 11?

Muraenosaurus waved its neck around, searching for food. Spot two.

Ophthalmosaurus had huge eyes to help it see underwater. Find three more.

Pholidophorus looked like a herring. Find 18.

Rhamphorhynchus scooped up fish in its beak. Find three.

Scaphognathus used its long tail to help it fly. Spot three.

Giant Liopleurodon was a very fast swimmer. Try finding two.

15

Cretaceous creatures

This scene shows some of the creatures that lived in Southern England during the early Cretaceous period. At the end of this period, about 65 million years ago, all the dinosaurs died out.

Dragonflies darted through the air. Try to find six.

Pelorosaurus lumbered over the plains. Spot seven.

Hylaeosaurus was covered with knobs and spikes. Find three.

Early seabirds flew overhead. Spot six.

Baryonyx scooped up fish to eat. Find three.

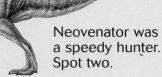

Neovenator was a speedy hunter. Spot two.

Hypsilophodon used its beak to snip at ferns. Find six.

Ornithocheirus was a flying reptile with huge, leathery wings. Find four more.

Beetles crawled over leaves. Can you see 14?

Bernissartia was a tiny crocodile. Find five.

Early mammals scurried over the ground. Spot three of each kind.

Pond tortoises lived close to the water. Find six.

Vectisaurus had a ridge along its back. Can you see three?

Polacanthus was protected by bony plates and spines. Spot four.

Iguanodon had a large spike on its thumb. Spot six more.

After the dinosaurs

After the dinosaurs died out, many new mammals developed. Some were large and lumbering, but others were small and speedy. Climbing mammals lived in trees and early bats flew through the air.

Uintatherium was a massive creature with a very knobbly head. Find two.

Coryphodon loved to splash around in water. Spot four.

Patriofelis looked like a small panther. Can you see three?

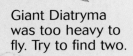

Giant Diatryma was too heavy to fly. Try to find two.

Pristichampsus was a crocodile that lived on land. Spot two.

Stylinodon dug up roots to eat. Find five.

Icaronycteris was an early bat. Spot 12 more.

Champsosaurus caught fish in its long jaws. Find three.

Smilodectes could leap from branch to branch. Spot seven more.

Diacodexis was a fast runner. Can you see nine?

Ischyromys climbed trees like a squirrel. Spot three.

Lively Chriacus scampered around, eating insects and fruit. Find four.

Hyrachyus was an ancestor of the rhino. Spot four.

Tiny Hyracotherium was the first horse. Find six more.

Lizards and snakes slithered through the forest. Spot four of each.

19

In South America

Around 150 million years ago, South America became an island. It stayed cut off from the rest of the world for the next 145 million years. Some of its animals were unlike creatures anywhere else.

Peltephilus was covered with bony plates. Try to find two.

Rabbit-like Protypotherium bounded over the grassy plains. Spot five.

Large water snakes waited for their prey. Can you spot three?

Eocardia was a good swimmer. It lived near rivers and ponds. Find four.

Homalodotherium liked eating leaves. Sometimes it prowled around on all fours. Find two more.

Hapalops often hung upside-down from tree branches. Try to find three.

Homunculus could wrap its tail around branches. Can you spot six?

Butterflies flitted through the grasslands. Try finding 17 more.

Necrolestes used its nose to help find insects to eat. Find two.

Astrapotherium lived on water plants. Can you see three?

Graceful Thoatherium looked like a small gazelle. Try to find nine.

Cladosictis hunted fish, reptiles and mice. Can you spot six?

Diadiaphorus looked like a very small horse. Try to find nine.

Theosodon had legs like a camel and a long nose. Can you spot four?

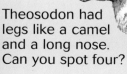

Phorusrhacos could run fast but couldn't fly. Find two.

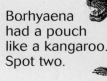

Borhyaena had a pouch like a kangaroo. Spot two.

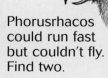

21

African animals

During the Miocene epoch, some very large animals lived in Africa. Early elephants roamed over the grassland, and hippos and rhinos wallowed in rivers. Can you find 70 African creatures?

Giant hippos splashed around in rivers. Spot six.

Vultures flew overhead, searching for food. Find five more.

Dendropithecus swung through the trees. Can you see five?

Sivapithecus could stand on its hind legs. Spot six.

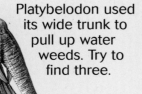

Platybelodon used its wide trunk to pull up water weeds. Try to find three.

Kanuites lived in trees as well as on the ground. Spot five.

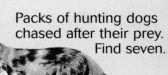

Packs of hunting dogs chased after their prey. Find seven.

Teleoceras was an early rhino. Find two.

Aardvarks rooted around for insects to eat. Spot three.

Deinotherium was a giant elephant with downward-curving tusks. Find two.

Prolibytherium had big horns but was actually an early giraffe. Spot six.

Early ostriches could run very fast. Find four.

Tree snakes hung from branches. Spot four.

Afrosmilus was a cunning hunter that could climb trees. Can you spot two?

Hipparion was an early horse. Spot seven.

Percrocuta fed on dead animals. Find four more.

A sticky end

Around 20,000 years ago, many creatures in California drowned in pits of tar. Others came to feed on them, but they became stuck as well. Here are some of the animals that drowned in the pits.

Herds of bison wandered over the grasslands. Can you see 10?

Camelops looked like a modern llama. Spot four.

Teratorns fed on dead and dying animals. Find six.

Western horses were smaller than horses today. Spot eight.

Giant sloths had bony lumps under their skins. Find two.

Weasels raced through the long grass. Spot five.

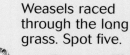

Eagles swooped down on their prey. Can you see four?

24

Frogs and toads were trapped in tar. Find three of each.

Frog

Toad

Rattlesnakes could make their tails vibrate. Try to spot three.

Smilodon had huge, curved fangs. Spot two more.

Dire wolves hunted in packs. Can you see six?

Male turkey

Male turkeys had splendid feathers. Find three females and two males.

Female turkey

Storks flew in to join the feast. Find four.

Mammoths used their tusks to shovel up food. Spot six.

Icy wastes

During the Earth's long history, there have been several ice ages. At these times, large parts of the globe were covered by ice and snow. This scene is set in Russia during the last ice age.

Megaloceros was the largest deer that has ever lived. Spot three.

Great auks were birds that could swim. Can you see 12?

Arctic foxes were cunning hunters. Find three more.

Lemmings dug tunnels in the snow. Spot seven.

Bears often sheltered inside caves. Find three.

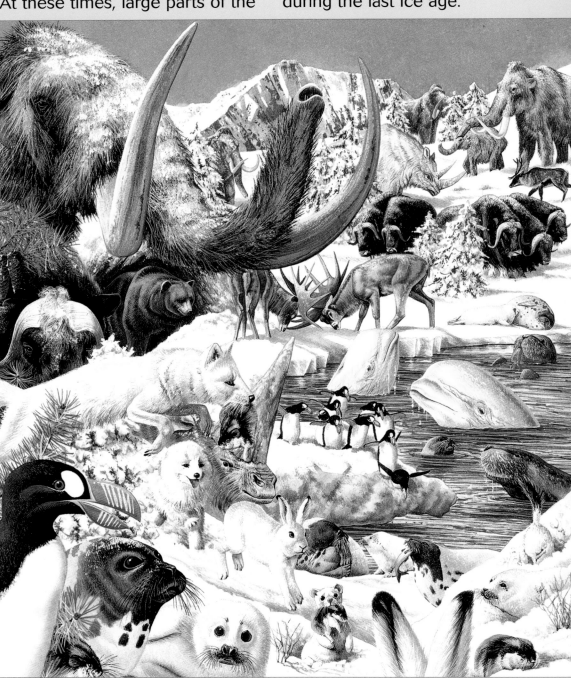

Sea cows had a layer of blubber to keep them warm. Find two.

Woolly rhinos were covered with thick hair. Spot two.

Enormous whales plunged through the icy water. Spot two.

Woolly mammoths had a store of fat on their heads. Find five more.

Seals gave birth to fluffy white pups. Find five adults and four pups.

Arctic hares were hard to spot against the snow. Spot five.

Shaggy musk oxen roamed over the snow. Try to find six.

Reindeer fought off hunters with their horns. Find 11 more.

Arctic stoats could squeeze through tunnels after their prey. Spot four.

Elasmotherium had a huge horn made from hair. Find one more.

Prehistoric puzzles

Why not test your prehistoric knowledge by trying out these puzzles? You will probably need to look back through the book to find out the answers. If you are really stuck, you can look on page 32.

1. All these dinosaurs except one hunted animals. Spot the plant-eater.

A B C D E

2. One of these creatures is not a bird. Do you know which one it is?

A B C D E

3. Can you guess which of these creatures is not a dinosaur?

A B C D E

Answers

The keys on the next few pages show you exactly where all the animals and plants appear in the scenes in this book. You can use these keys if you have a problem trying to find a particular creature or plant.

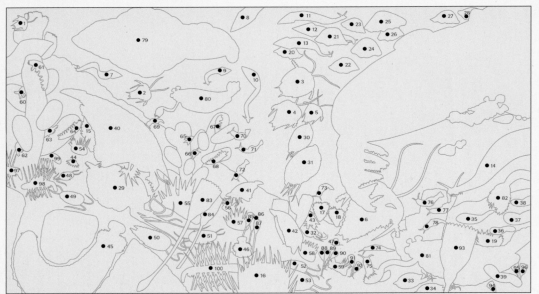

Crowded seas 8–9

Marrella 1 2 3 4 5 6	Dinomischus 83 84
Pikaia 7 8 9 10 11	85 86 87 88 89
12 13 14	90 91 92 93 94
Sponges 15 16 17	95 96
18 19	Hallucigenia 97 98
Jellyfish 20 21	99 100
22 23 24 25 26	
27 28	
Leanchoilia 29 30	
31 32 33 34	
Odontogriphus 35	
36 37 38 39	
Sanctacaris 40 41	
42 43	
Ottoia 44 45 46 47	
Trilobites 48 49 50	
51 52 53	
Wiwaxia 54 55 56	
57 58 59	
Aysheaia 60 61	
62 63 64 65 66	
67 68	
Amiskwia 69 70 71	
72 73 74 75 76	
77 78	
Anomalocaris 79	
Opabinia 80 81 82	

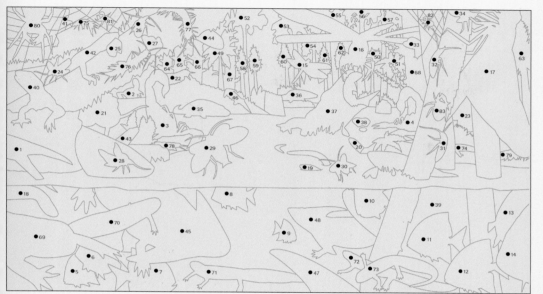

Forests and swamps 10–11

Giant scorpions 1 2
 3 4
Platysomus 5 6
 7 8 9 10 11 12
 13 14
Meganeura 15
 16 17
Ophiderpeton 18
 19 20
Arthropleura 21
 22 23
Cockroaches 24
 25 26 27 28 29
 30 31 32 33 34
Eryops 35 36 37
 38 39
Hylonomus 40 41
 42 43 44
Diploceraspis 45 46
 47 48
Tree ferns 49
 50 51
Lepidodendron
 52 53 54 55
 56 57
Sigillaria 58 59 60
 61 62 63
Giant horsetails 64
 65 66 67 68

Keraterpeton 69 70
 71 72 73 74
Centipedes 75 76
 77 78 79
Spiders 80 81
 82 83

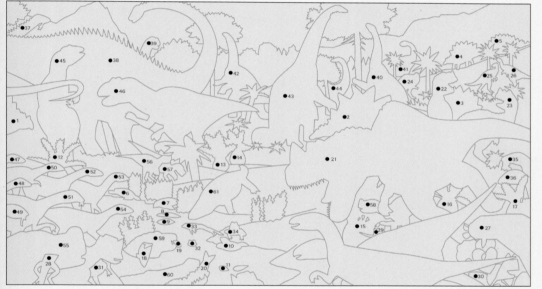

Jurassic giants 12–13

Stegosaurus 1 2 3
 4 5
Turtles 6 7 8 9
 10 11
Cycads 12 13 14
 15 16 17
Lepidotes 18 19 20
Ceratosaurus 21
 22 23
Camptosaurus 24 25
 26 27
Lizards 28 29 30
Frogs 31 32 33 34
Dryosaurus 35 36
Diplodocus 37 38
Camarasaurus 39
 40 41
Apatosaurus 42
 43 44
Allosaurus 45 46
Othnielia 47 48 49
 50 51 52 53 54
Ornitholestes 55
 56 57 58
Goniopholis 59
 60 61

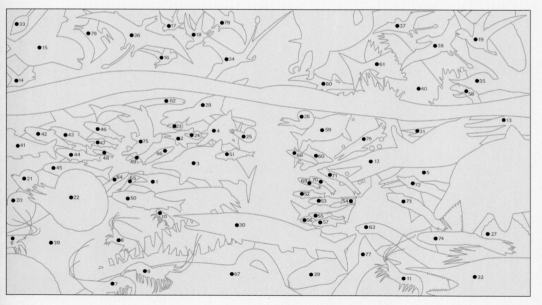

Oceans and skies 14–15

Ichthyosaurus 1 2 3
 4 5
Shrimps 6 7 8 9
 10 11
Peloneustes 12 13
Anurognathus 14 15
 16 17 18 19
Ammonites 20
 21 22 23 24
 25 26 27
Cryptoclidus 28 29
Aspidorhynchus 30
 31 32
Rhamphorhynchus
 33 34 35
Scaphognathus 36
 37 38
Liopleurodon 39 40
Pholidophorus 41
 42 43 44 45 46
 47 48 49 50 51
 52 53 54 55 56
 57 58
Ophthalmosaurus 59
 60 61
Muraenosaurus
 62 63

Belemnites 64
 65 66 67 68 69
 70 71 72 73 74
Metriorhynchus 75
 76 77
Pterodactylus 78
 79 80

29

Cretaceous creatures 16–17

Dragonflies 1 2 3 4
  5 6
Pelorosaurus 7 8 9
  10 11 12 13
Hylaeosaurus 14
  15 16
Seabirds 17 18 19
  20 21 22
Baryonyx 23 24 25
Neovenator 26 27
Hypsilophodon 28
  29 30 31 32 33
Vectisaurus 34
  35 36
Polacanthus 37 38
  39 40
Iguanodon 41 42
  43 44 45 46
Pond tortoises 47 48
  49 50 51 52
Mammals 53 54 55
  56 57 58
Bernissartia 59 60
  61 62 63
Beetles 64 65 66 67
  68 69 70 71 72
  73 74 75 76 77

Ornithocheirus 78
  79 80 81

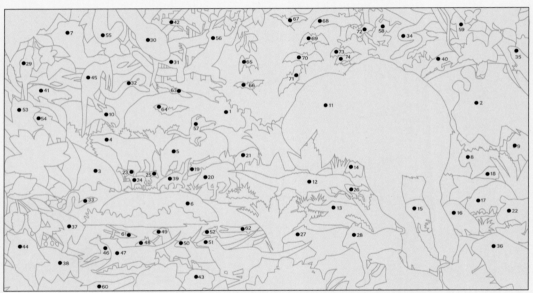

After the dinosaurs 18–19

Uintatherium 1 2
Coryphodon 3 4 5 6
Patriofelis 7 8 9
Diatryma 10 11
Pristichampsus 12 13
Stylinodon 14 15 16
  17 18
Hyrachyus 19 20
  21 22
Hyracotherium 23
  24 25 26 27 28
Lizards and snakes
  29 30 31 32 33
  34 35 36
Chriacus 37 38
  39 40
Ischyromys 41
  42 43
Diacodexis 44 45
  46 47 48 49 50
  51 52
Smilodectes 53 54
  55 56 57 58 59
Champsosaurus 60
  61 62
Icaronycteris 63 64
  65 66 67 68 69
  70 71 72 73 74

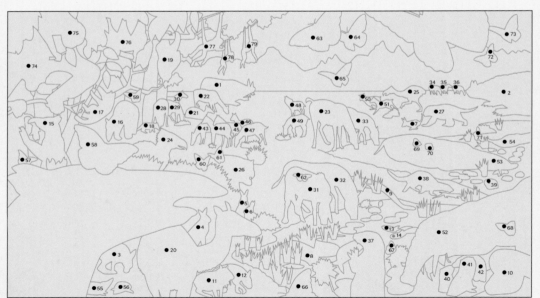

In South America 20–21

Peltephilus 1 2
Protypotherium 3 4
  5 6 7
Water snakes 8 9 10
Eocardia 11 12 13 14
Homalodotherium
  15 16
Hapalops 17 18 19
Theosodon 20 21
  22 23
Phorusrhacos 24 25
Borhyaena 26 27
Diadiaphorus 28 29
  30 31 32 33 34
  35 36
Cladosictis 37 38 39
  40 41 42
Thoatherium 43 44
  45 46 47 48 49
  50 51
Astrapotherium 52
  53 54
Necrolestes 55 56
Butterflies 57 58 59
  60 61 62 63 64
  65 66 67 68 69
  70 71 72 73
Homunculus 74 75
  76 77 78 79

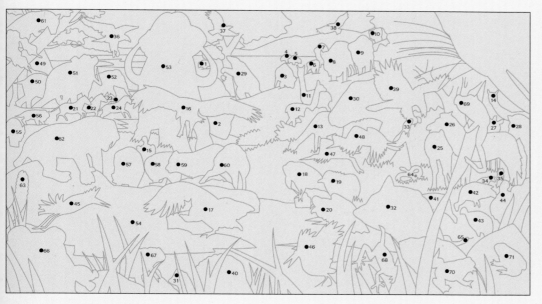

African animals 22–23

Hippos 1 2 3 4
5 6
Vultures 7 8 9 10 11
Dendropithecus 12
13 14 15 16
Sivapithecus 17 18
19 20 21 22
Platybelodon 23
24 25
Kanuites 26 27 28
29 30
Hunting dogs 31 32
33 34 35 36 37
Hipparion 38 39
40 41 42 43 44
Afrosmilus 45 46
Percrocuta 47 48
49 50
Tree snakes 51 52
53 54
Early ostriches 55
56 57 58
Prolibytherium 59
60 61 62 63 64
Deinotherium 65 66
Aardvarks 67 68 69
Teleoceras 70 71

A sticky end 24–25

Bison 1 2 3 4 5 6 7
8 9 10
Camelops 11 12
13 14
Teratorns 15 16 17
18 19 20
Western horses 21
22 23 24 25 26
27 28
Giant sloths 29 30
Weasels 31 32 33
34 35
Eagles 36 37
38 39
Turkeys 40 41 42
43 44
Storks 45 46
47 48
Mammoths 49 50
51 52 53 54
Dire wolves 55 56
57 58 59 60
Smilodon 61 62
Rattlesnakes 63
64 65
Frogs and toads 66
67 68 69 70 71

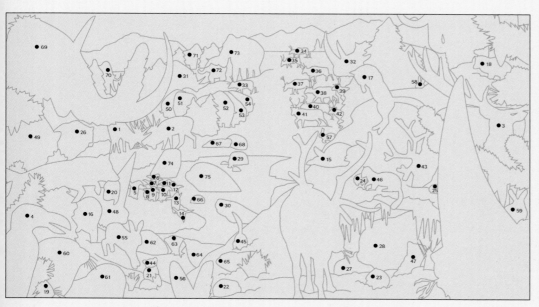

Icy wastes 26–27

Megaloceros 1 2 3
Great auks 4 5 6 7
8 9 10 11 12 13
14 15
Arctic foxes 16
17 18
Lemmings 19 20
21 22 23 24 25
Bears 26 27 28
Sea cows 29 30
Woolly rhinos 31 32
Reindeer 33 34 35
36 37 38 39 40
41 42 43
Arctic stoats 44 45
46 47
Elasmotherium 48
Musk oxen 49 50 51
52 53 54
Arctic hares 55 56
57 58 59
Seals 60 61 62 63
64 65 66 67 68
Woolly mammoths
69 70 71 72 73
Whales 74 75

Index

Cover design: Zoe Wray.
Additional illustration: Inklink Firenze.
Picture credit: p7, ©Digital Vision.

Answers to prehistoric puzzles: 1. **D** Camarasaurus, 2. **B** Anurognathus, 3. **D** Peloneustes

THE HAPPY PRINCE

High above the city, on a tall column, stood the statue of the Happy Prince. He was gilded all over with thin leaves of fine gold, for eyes he had two bright sapphires, and a large red ruby glowed on his sword-hilt.

He was very much admired indeed. "He is as beautiful as a weathercock," remarked one of the Town Councillors who wished to gain a reputation for having artistic tastes, "only not quite so useful," he added, fearing lest people should think him un-practical, which he really was not.

"He looks just like an angel," said the Charity Children as they came out of the cathedral in their bright scarlet cloaks and clean white pinafores.

"How do you know?" said the Mathematical Master. "You have never seen one."

"Ah! But we have, in our dreams," answered the children; and the Mathematical Master frowned, for he did not approve of children dreaming.

One night there flew over the city a little Swallow. His friends had gone away to Egypt six weeks before, but he had stayed behind, for he was in love with the most beautiful Reed. He had met her in the spring as he was flying down the river after a big yellow moth, and had been so attracted that he had stopped to talk to her.

"Shall I love you?" said the Swallow, who liked to come to the point at once, and the Reed made him a low bow. So he flew round and round her, touching the water with his wings, and making silver ripples. This was his courtship, and it lasted all through the summer.

"It is a ridiculous attach-ment," twittered the other Swallows. "She has no money, and far too many relations." And indeed the river was quite full of Reeds. Then, when the autumn came they all flew away.

After they had gone he felt lonely, and began to tire of his ladylove. "She has no conversa-tion," he said, "and I am afraid that she is a coquette, for she is always flirting with the wind. I admit that she is domestic, but I love travelling, and my wife, consequently, should love travelling also."

"Will you come away with me?" he said finally to her, but the Reed shook her head.

"You have been trifling with me," he cried. "I am off to the Pyramids. Good-bye!" and he flew away.

All day long he flew, and at night-time he arrived at the city and saw the statue on the tall column.

"I will put up there," he cried, "it is a fine position, with plenty of fresh air." So he alighted just between the feet of the Happy Prince.

"I have a golden bedroom," he said softly to himself as he looked round, and he prepared to go to sleep; but just as he was putting his head under his wing a large drop of water fell on him. "What a curious thing!" he cried, "there is not a single cloud in the sky, the stars are quite clear and bright, yet it is raining."

Another drop fell.

"What is the use of a statue if it cannot keep the rain off?" he said. And he determined to fly away.

But before he had opened his wings a third drop fell, and he looked up and saw . . . Ah! What did he see?

The eyes of the Happy Prince were filled with tears, and tears were running down his golden cheeks. His face was so beautiful in the moonlight that the little Swallow was filled with pity.

"Who are you?" he said.

"I am the Happy Prince."

"Why are you weeping then?" asked the Swallow. "You have quite drenched me."

"When I was alive and had a human heart," answered the statue, "I did not know what tears were, for I lived in the Palace of Sans-Souci, where sorrow is not allowed to enter.

"Round the garden ran a very lofty wall, but I never cared to ask what lay beyond it, everything about me was so beautiful. My courtiers called me the Happy Prince, and happy indeed I was, if pleasure be happiness. So I lived, and so I died. And now that I am dead they have set me up here so high that I can see all the ugliness and all the misery of my city, and though my heart is made of lead yet I cannot choose but weep."

"Far away," continued the statue in a low musical voice, "far away in a little street there is a poor house. One of the windows is open, and through it I can see a woman seated at a table. Her face is thin and worn, and she has coarse, red hands, all pricked by the needle, for she is a seamstress. She is embroidering a satin gown for the next Court-ball. In a bed in the corner of the room her little boy is lying ill. He has a fever, and is asking for oranges. His mother has nothing to give him but water, so he is crying. Swallow, Swallow, little Swallow, will you not bring her the ruby out of my sword-hilt? My feet are fastened to this pedestal and I cannot move."

"I am waited for in Egypt," said the Swallow. "My friends are flying up and down the Nile, and talking to the large lotus-flowers. Soon they will go to sleep in the tomb of the great King. The King is there himself in his painted coffin. He is wrapped in yellow linen, and embalmed with spices. Round his neck is a chain of pale green jade, and his hands are like withered leaves."

"Swallow, Swallow, little Swallow," said the Prince, "will you not stay with me for one night, and be my messenger? The boy is so thirsty, and the mother so sad."

"I don't think I like boys," answered the Swallow. "Last summer, when I was staying on the river, there were two rude boys who were always throwing stones at me. They never hit me, of course; we swallows fly far too well for that, and besides, I come of a family famous for its agility; but still, it was a mark of disrespect."

But the Happy Prince looked so sad that the little Swallow was sorry. "It is very cold here," he said; "but I will stay with you for one night, and be your messenger."

So the Swallow picked out the great ruby from the Prince's sword, and flew away with it in his beak over the roofs of the town.

He passed by the cathedral tower, where the white marble angels were sculptured. He passed by the palace and heard the sound of dancing.

He passed over the river, and saw the lanterns hanging to the masts of the ships. He passed over the Ghetto, and saw the old Jews bargaining with each other, and weighing out money in copper scales.

At last he came to the poor house. The boy was tossing feverishly on his bed, and the mother had fallen asleep, she was so tired. In he hopped, and laid the great ruby on the table beside the woman's thimble. Then he flew gently round the bed, fanning the boy's forehead with his wings. "How cool I feel!" said the boy, and he sank into a delicious slumber.

Then the Swallow flew back to the Happy Prince, and told him what he had done. "It is curious," he remarked, "but I feel quite warm now, although it is so cold."

"That's because you have done a good action," said the Prince.

When day broke the Swallow flew down to the river and had a bath. "What a remarkable phenomenon!" said the Professor of Ornithology as he was passing. "A swallow in winter!" And he wrote a long letter about it to the local newspaper. Every one quoted it, it was full of so many words that they could not understand.

When the moon rose the Swallow flew back to the Happy Prince. "Have you any commissions for Egypt?" he cried, "I am just starting."

"Swallow, Swallow, little Swallow," said the Prince, "will you not stay with me one night longer?"

"I am waited for in Egypt," answered the Swallow. "To-morrow my friends will fly up to the Second Cataract. At noon the yellow lions come down to the water's edge to drink. They have eyes like green beryls, and their roar is

louder than the roar of the cataract."

"Swallow, Swallow, little Swallow," said the Prince, "far away across the city I see a young man in a garret. He is leaning over a desk covered with papers, and in a tumbler by his side there is a bunch of withered violets. His hair is brown and crisp, and his lips are red as a pomegranate, and he has large and dreamy eyes. He is trying to finish a play but he is too cold to write any more. There is no fire in the grate, and hunger has made him faint."

"I will wait with you one night longer," said the Swallow, who really had a good heart. "Shall I take him another ruby?"

"Alas! I have no ruby now," said the Prince, "my eyes are all that I have left. They are made of rare sapphires, which were brought out of India a thousand years ago. Pluck out one of them and take it to him. He will sell it to buy firewood and finish his play."

"Dear Prince," said the Swallow, "I cannot do that." And he began to weep.

"Swallow, Swallow, little Swallow," said the Prince, "do as I command you."

So the Swallow plucked out the Prince's eye, and flew away to the student's garret. It was easy enough to get in, as there was a hole in the roof. Through this he darted, and came into the room. The young man had his head buried in his hands, so he did not hear the flutter of the bird's wings, and when he looked up he found the beautiful sapphire lying on the withered violets.

The next day the Swallow flew down to the harbour. He sat on the mast of a large vessel and watched the sailors hauling big chests out of the hold with ropes, and when the moon rose he flew back to the Happy Prince.

"I am come to bid you good-bye," he cried.

"Swallow, Swallow, little Swallow," said the Prince, "will you not stay with me one night longer?"

"It is winter," answered the Swallow, "and the chill snow will soon be here. In Egypt the sun is warm on the green palm-trees, and the crocodiles lie in the mud and look lazily about them. Dear Prince, I must leave you, but I will never forget you, and next spring I will bring you back two beautiful jewels in place of those you have given away. The ruby shall be redder than a red rose, and the sapphire shall be as blue as the great sea."

"In the square below," said the Happy Prince, "is a little match-girl. She has let her matches fall in the gutter, and they are all spoiled. Her father will beat her if she brings home no money,

and she is crying. She has no shoes or stockings, and her little head is bare. Pluck out my other eye, and give it to her, and her father will not beat her."

"I will stay with you one night longer," said the Swallow, "but I cannot pluck out your eye. You would be quite blind then."

"Swallow, Swallow, little Swallow," said the Prince, "do as I command you."

So he plucked out the Prince's other eye, swooped past the match-girl, and slipped the jewel into the palm of her hand. "What a lovely bit of glass!" cried the little girl; and she ran home, laughing.

Then the Swallow came back to the Prince. "You are blind now," he said, "so I will stay with you always."

"No, little Swallow," said the poor Prince, "you must go away to Egypt."

"I will stay with you always," said the Swallow, and he slept at the Prince's feet.

All the next day he sat on the Prince's shoulder, and told him stories of strange lands. He told him of the red ibises who stand in long rows on the banks of the Nile and catch goldfish in their beaks; of the Sphinx who is as old as the world itself and knows everything; of the merchants who walk slowly by the side of their camels and carry amber beads in their hands; of the King of the Mountains of the Moon who is as black as ebony and worships a large crystal and of the pygmies who sail over a big lake on large flat leaves and are always at war with the butterflies.

"Dear little Swallow," said the Prince, "you tell me of marvellous things, but more marvellous than anything is the suffering of men and of women. There is no Mystery so great as Misery. Fly over my city, little Swallow, and tell me what you see there."

So the Swallow flew over the great city and saw the rich making merry in their beautiful houses while the beggars were sitting at the gates. He flew into dark lanes and saw the white faces of starving children looking out listlessly at the black streets.

Then he flew back and told the Prince what he had seen.

"I am covered with fine gold," said the Prince. Take

it off, leaf by leaf, and give it to my poor; the living always think that gold can make them happy."

Leaf after leaf of the fine gold the Swallow picked off, till the Happy Prince looked quite dull and grey. Leaf after leaf of the fine gold he brought to the poor, and the children's faces grew rosier and they laughed and played games in the street.

Then the snow came, and after the snow came the frost. The streets looked as if they were made of silver, they were so bright and glistening; long icicles like crystal daggers hung down from the eaves of the houses, everybody went about in furs, and the little boys wore scarlet caps and skated on the ice.

The poor little Swallow grew colder and colder, but he would not leave the Prince, he loved him too well. He picked up crumbs outside the baker's door, and tried to keep himself warm by flapping his wings.

But at last he knew that he was going to die. He has just enough strength to fly up to the Prince's shoulder. "Good-bye, dear Prince!" he murmured, "will you let me kiss your hand?"

"I am glad you are going to Egypt at last, little Swallow," said the Prince, "you have stayed too long here; but you must kiss me on the lips, for I love you."

"It is not to Egypt that I am going," said the Swallow. "I am going to the House of Death. Death is the brother of Sleep, is he not?"

And he kissed the Happy Prince on the lips, and fell down dead at his feet.

At that moment a curious crack sounded inside the statue, as if something had broken. The fact is that the leaden heart had snapped right in two.

Early the next morning the Mayor was walking in the square in company with the Town Councillors. As they passed he looked up at the statue: "Dear me! How shabby the Happy Prince looks!" he said. "The ruby has fallen out of his sword, his eyes are gone, and he is golden no longer. In fact, he is little better than a beggar!"

"Little better than a beggar," said the Town Councillors, who always agreed with the Mayor.

"And here is actually a dead bird at his feet!" continued the Mayor. "We must really issue a proclamation that birds are not to be allowed to die here."

So they pulled down the statue of the Happy Prince. "As he is no longer beautiful he is no longer useful," said the Art Professor at the University.

Then they melted the statue in a furnace.

"What a strange thing!" said the overseer of the workmen at the foundry. "This broken lead heart will not melt in the furnace. We must throw it away." So they threw it on a dust-heap where the dead Swallow was also lying.

"Bring me the two most precious things in the city," said God to one of His Angels; and the Angel brought Him the leaden heart and the dead bird.

"You have rightly chosen," said God, "for in my garden of Paradise this little bird shall sing for evermore, and in my city of gold the Happy Prince shall praise me."